GOD IS PRETTY GOOD AT SECOND CHANCES

Cover design by Sara Young
Cover photo by James Robinson

ISBN: 978-1-962401-30-2   1 2 3 4 5 6 7 8 9 10

Printed in the United States of America

GOD IS PRETTY GOOD AT SECOND CHANCES

MY PERSONAL STORY

RAQUEL COPELAND

DREAM RELEASER PUBLISHING

*I am dedicating this book to my late
mother, Georgia Emerson, and my late
grandmothers, Nettie Highshaw and
Virginia Emerson. You are among my
cloud of witnesses who have watched
over me my entire life and guided
me in the writing of this book.*

CONTENTS

Acknowledgments ix

Introduction. 11

CHAPTER 1. **Motherless: Triumph over Trauma** 15

CHAPTER 2. **A Twenty-Year Journey**

　　　　　　for a Four-Year Degree .33

CHAPTER 3. **Paycheck or Purpose** 47

CHAPTER 4. **The Call and the Response**. 57

CHAPTER 5. **Divorced but Not Denied Love**. 71

CHAPTER 6. **Blooming: God Made Dirt**

　　　　　　and Dirt Don't Hurt. 81

Haikus—September 2021 89

ACKNOWLEDGMENTS

First, I acknowledge my children. I am thankful for my three heartbeats, Brianna, Jerrode, and Brandon. Each of you inspire me in your own unique way. You've seen me at my worst, and now you're seeing me at my best. And through it all, you've never given up on me. I love you all so very much.

I acknowledge my Aunts: Bessie, Helen, Charlotte, Peggy, Diane, May, Joyce, and Debra. You have been instrumental in shaping me to be the woman I am today. (Aunts Zee, Shirley, Faye, and Michelle, continue to rest in heaven.)

I also acknowledge the best friends, queen sisters, and accountability partners a girl could ever have: Earlina, Stacey, and Tiffany. We are REST forever. To my mentor, my spiritual advisor, my girlfriend, Dawn. Thank you for always reminding me that my latter will be greater.

Last, and certainly not least, I want to acknowledge my loving husband, Tim. You have supported this project from inception to completion. Thank you for loving me with the love of God.

Father God, here is my story. You've helped me to write it; now use it for your glory. In Jesus' name. Amen.

INTRODUCTION

For a few years, I have been entertained by the thought of writing a book. I was really good at journaling, so I thought writing should be easy. I quickly discovered that while journaling was easy, writing a book was on another level of creativity. Journaling was for me. It was a way to get my thoughts on paper. Writing a book was for others, and this task was not easy for me at all. This task required a level of vulnerability that I was not sure I was ready to expose. But God said otherwise, so here I am.

In September 2021, I went on a five-day camping trip. One day after lunch, I was relaxing in my reclining chair, and I began to observe everything around me . . . everything, being nature. The thought "write a haiku about what you see" came. And so, the writing began. Now, the haikus did not follow the exact format of the traditional haiku; nevertheless, my creativity awakened, and within two days I had written sixteen haiku poems.

The more I observed different aspects of nature, the more inspired I became to write. I paid attention to the grass and shrubbery, and every so often there was a pop of color from a small flower. I watched the ants go about their day, and the squirrels as they played and gathered their food. I watched how the trees swayed back and forth as if they were in worship.

Later in the evening, I observed how the spiders crafted their webs. The sparks from the campfire drew me in as I thought about the burning desire to become an author. And then there were the nightly storms that put fear in me until I realized who controlled the winds and the rain.

The more I allowed nature to speak to me, the more I began to understand my writing assignment: Creation is a part of God's story. What's my story?

In this book, you will see several journeys that I have taken throughout my life and witness how God orchestrated second chances, even when I didn't see the second chance until years later. My prayer is that something you read will inspire and encourage you to look at your own life and begin to embrace the second chance God has given you. Too often we dwell on our pain and failures, and we miss what is in front of us. We miss the fact that God is really good at second chances.

CHAPTER I

MOTHERLESS: TRIUMPH OVER TRAUMA

Empty beginnings.
What was. What is. What can be.
Latter is greater.

I felt the hand of someone waking me up from a night of sleep. "Raquel, wake up", the voice said. It was the voice of my father. I woke up and saw him standing there. "Your mom has died" is all I remember, and so the void began. . . .

A motherless child. Not because she didn't want me. Not because she didn't love me. But because her journey on earth had ended and God called her home. I don't remember much of my mother. I was a toddler when she became ill, and she died when I was just eight years old.

A life without a mother left me with a lot of "I wonders". I wonder what I would be like today, at this very moment, if I was raised by my mother. I wonder if she would be proud of me. I wonder what she would be like as a grandmother and a great-grandmother. I wonder what her spirituality would be like today. What was her favorite color? Her favorite song? Her favorite flower? I wonder if she had a love for nature like I do. Hmmm . . . I wondered and still wonder.

Life without a mother meant I didn't have anyone to call Mommy, or Mom, or Mama. I didn't have a mother to share my first menstruation with, or to tell about my first crush. She wasn't there for mommy and daughter time. After all, I am the only girl. I didn't have her at my eighth-grade graduation, high school graduation, or even college graduation. I didn't have a mother to celebrate my milestone birthdays. I didn't have her to make wedding plans or to watch the joy in her face as she held her grandchildren. I always yearned to experience having someone to talk to about personal stuff . . . someone to talk to about nothing at all . . . someone to just hang out with . . . someone like a mother.

A void to never be filled. No one can ever fill the empty space of a mother. I had to grow up watching everyone else enjoy their mothers. I got to watch all my friends and cousins interact with their own mothers, only to wish I had that same opportunity . . . a wish upon the stars, a wish just before blowing out birthday candles, a wish just before blowing the puffball on a dandelion . . . a wish never to come true. I have been told I look like her and at times behave like her. I have been told I carry her mannerisms, and I even love basketball as she did. The stories are great, but her absence will never let me experience her firsthand.

One could say that, from the outside, I looked fine. But you could never imagine what life was like on the inside. There was so much hidden anger, resentment, envy, and jealousy. There was also a great sadness and longing on the inside of me and great sadness and longing that I still carry with me today. I would get so angry when I saw children disrespecting their mothers. I recall an incident where one of my cousins showed disrespect to her mother, evoking intense emotions in me and a strong inclination to address the situation. My feelings of distress weren't solely about her disrespecting her mother; they were more connected to her seeming unawareness of the privilege of having a mother. As I sat there without my own mom, the stark contrast struck me deeply–she dared to mistreat hers. The strong urge to suggest, "Okay, let's resolve this through a fight," surfaced prominently.

I always remember being a happy-go-lucky child. A child full of optimism, always seeing the good in people. I participated in many activities in my youth. I played basketball and volleyball; I was a cheerleader and member of the pom-pom squad. I was a member of the forensics team, and in high school, I was part of the H.E.R.O. club, which allowed me to have half-days in my senior year and work the other half. I was in school plays, and I participated in church events. The summers were always full as I attended summer camps and then Vacation Bible School in the evenings. All the fun and excitement only to lay down at night wondering, "Who will wake me up to tell me my grandmother died?" Great joy during the day . . . great sadness at night as I lay in the bed and wept silent tears.

I have carried this great sadness all of my life. Along with this sadness were secret anger and envy. Why was I angry, you ask? Well, I felt that God robbed me of the most precious thing a girl could have . . . her mother. Why was I envious of others? You've probably figured that out already. My cousins, friends, neighborhood kids . . . everyone had their mommy except me. Regardless of the relationship between them and their mothers, the fact of the matter is that they had their mothers. Someone to call Mom.

Being a motherless child is where it all began—being a part of something yet feeling alone. The feeling of rejection and abandonment, and the fear of being abandoned yet again. The envy of mother-daughter relationships. The insecure attachments with the ease of detaching, disconnecting, and withdrawing all at the same time. All of this internal decay while maintaining a smile and portraying a calm demeanor, a sense of joy and peace, and a "put-togetherness" persona. Years and years of despising Mother's Day. I couldn't even appreciate the celebration of my own motherhood on this special day.

The void of a mother may come from the death of a mother, adoption, or broken relationships due to addictions or abuse. The point is not the how but that the void exists, and that can be detrimental, especially if not recognized. At least it was for me for most of my life. I was well into my forties before I understood the root of my behavior as well as the root of rejection and abandonment. I spent a lot of years cutting down branch after branch but never getting to the root. Author Kelly McDaniel coined it best as "mother hunger".[1]

I blamed my insecurities on my father; however, when I began to pull back layers, I recognized that I lost nurturance and protection from my own mother. I didn't have the bond from a mother, nor did I have her guidance. And because of that, those insecure

---

1 Kelly McDaniel, *Mother Hunger: How Adult Daughters Can Understand and Heal from Lost Nurturance, Protection, and Guidance* (Carlsbad, CA: Hay House, 2021).

attachments developed early in life. In pulling back the layers, I also recognized that I had not only lived with hidden anger and envy, but I also lived in a lot of secrecy and shame for the choices and mistakes I made.

I had such a yearning for love and belonging, so it's not a real shock that I got married and started a family at the young tender age of eighteen. I needed to belong, I needed affection, and I needed security. I give credit to those three needs . . . credit to the many insecure relationships I had with men, girlfriends, alcohol, and food. This unnamed issue, which was the root of my behavior, impacted my relationship with my own children, especially in their adult life. My own insecurities made my children feel unloved, unsupported, and unprotected. And so there again came the feelings of rejection, this time my own children's, only to realize that my insecurities were driving my behaviors and pushing them away.

The lack of nurture and protection from my mother caused me to struggle with making long-term friendships and loneliness. I could be in a room full of people, yet still feel like I was by myself or invisible. I so easily detached from people that I used to question whether I really cared for the person at all. Little did

I know that, subconsciously, I didn't get too attached for fear of people leaving me first. Enter the twins: rejection and abandonment.

That touch, affection, and warmth from a mother is nowhere in my memory. I don't remember my mother ever holding me, so I certainly don't remember her touch. The best way for me to get the touch I longed for, or thought I longed for, was from a man. Then, it became a man and food. And later it became a man, food, and alcohol. I thank God every day for keeping His hands on me because I put myself in some dangerous situations, and I could have easily eaten and drank myself crazy. But God!!

Not knowing this at the time, I now believe it's the foundation of God's love for me that allowed me to maintain a drive to overcome and not allow how I felt to overtake me. I had a choice—many choices as a child and later as an adult. I had a choice to be consumed by the sadness and anger of being a motherless child, which was my reality and my truth. I also had a choice to allow God to be what I heard but never understood: a mother to the motherless. I chose the latter, and this was my first time experiencing God as a God of second chances.

THERE WAS A VOID OF A MOTHER; HOWEVER, THERE WAS NEVER A VOID OF LOVE.

How did God show up in my life as "a mother to the motherless"? God took one mother and gave me ten mother figures. Talk about a ten-fold return!!! There was a void of a mother; however, there was never a void of love. My grandmothers and aunts loved me as their own daughter and gave me the nurturing, protection, and guidance that I needed to become the woman I am today. Of course, they did not and could never fill the void of Georgia Lee Emerson. However, it's because of them that I know what unconditional love feels like. My Madea, my mother's mother, was the epitome of all mothers. She taught me how to give unconditional love and tough love. Through her actions, she taught me how to pray and how to serve. She taught me how to be gentle and mild-mannered. Through her, I got to feel God's love and the tenderness and warm touch of a mother. I also had my Big Mama, my father's mother. It's through her that I got a second dose of the warm touch of a mother. And it's because of Big Mama that

I love oatmeal with raisins and cream of wheat to this day. My grandmothers taught me how to sacrifice, how to give, and how to serve others.

And then there were my aunts. I was blessed with twelve aunts, and two of them were more like my sisters. The other ten were more like mother figures, and each of them played a role in my childhood. Through them, I learned how to manage the affairs of my own home. Through Aunts Bessie, Charlotte, and Peggy, I learned family values and the importance of cooking, doing chores, and managing finances. I learned the importance of relationships, and I even learned how to overcome struggles. Today, as I go through struggles, I reflect on and remember a lot of the life lessons that my aunts taught me. For example, I am a "helper" by nature, and I recall my Auntie Big Joyce telling me, "Raquel, you can't save the world." Auntie Helen taught me that the world will never simply give things to me; I had to work hard for what I wanted and needed. Auntie Diane taught me that being silent is okay; it is okay to be still and let God. Auntie Charlotte taught me that cleanliness is next to godliness. And Auntie Peggy told me that when my mother died, I said to her, "That's okay, Auntie, mommy is not hurting anymore." Now, while I don't recall saying that to Auntie Peggy, I have used that to understand that God will heal how He chooses to heal.

A motherless child, but not a child without motherly care. I had love, care, and protection. Some become motherless later in life, but God chose me to become motherless as a child. I guess there were some things He needed to instill in me early that perhaps I would have taken for granted. I don't know, but what I do know is that while there will always be an empty space of a mother, there is never a lack of God filling that space with someone to care for me in the very moment that I need caring for. Even as I write, God has placed women in my life to care for me as a mother would to meet my current needs. God has been my mother through my grandmothers, aunts, and church mothers.

EMBRACE THE SADNESS AND HURT OR EMBRACE THE REDEEMING GOD WHO WILL BE WHAT YOU NEED AT EVERY MOMENT IN YOUR LIFE.

I will never know what it is like to have a mother journey with me in life. I will never know what it feels like to experience the death of a mother as an adult and then miss the times I have had with her. I don't know what it feels like to miss having conversations with my mother or to feel her touch. What I do know is that God gave me a second chance. And that second chance is what I choose to embrace. In this life, tragedy will happen, and we have a choice on what we will embrace. Embrace the sadness and hurt or embrace the redeeming God who will be what you need at every moment in your life. Sometimes, we can't get past a thing because to hold on to it is unconscious comfort and protection. In God's truth, that trauma can work out for your good if you let it. If you can see past the sting and allow yourself to step out of your reality, God can then step in and offer you that second chance. I am still working through the trauma, and probably will until I take my last breath. However, I choose triumph. Today, what will you choose?

PRAYER:

Father God, I ask that you give comfort to the one who feels a void in their life . . . the void of their mother. I ask that you give them the courage and boldness to step out of the reality and sting of not having their mother in the present, and welcome the embrace of the love, protection, and care from others that you have placed in their lives. You are indeed a mother to the motherless, so allow us to continue to see how you show up in others when the need for a touch or word from a mother arises. In Jesus' name. Amen.

JOURNAL ENTRY
February 26, 2018

And so it begins. My life as a little girl is blurred. I vaguely remember the homes that I lived in with my mother and siblings. As a matter of fact, I vaguely remember my mother, Georgia Lee Emerson. I have always had this scene in my head at a house on Concordia (I believe), and my mother was walking down the stairs and fell. I was between three to five years old. I vaguely remember going from house to house and being cared for, but

I never remember going to my father's house until I was much older. I do remember that at five years old we all moved in with Madea and Papa Daddy . . . me, my mother, and siblings, and that's because my mother was stricken with Multiple Sclerosis. I remember going to Oliver Windell Holmes for first grade, and in second grade I started attending St. Phillips Lutheran School.

At five years old, my life started at 3009 N. Richards Street in Milwaukee, WI. I remember seeing my mother lying in the hospital bed that was placed in the living room by the two windows. And at seven or eight years old, I remember being awakened by the news that my mother had passed away. I think I cried; I'm not really sure. I have this other scene in my head that I went to the Wake, and when I saw my mother lying there, I became speechless. Again, I don't know if I cried. I don't remember going to the funeral, and as I recall, the Wake was the last thing I remember about my mother.

I never asked questions, and I don't remember anyone ever talking to me about my mother. I remember being kept busy throughout my entire elementary school years. I went to St. Phillips/Beautiful Savior through the eighth grade. I was in school plays, the school choir, and church skits, and I was on the debate team. I was a cheerleader, and I played basketball and volleyball. I remember in the summers we would walk to parks to play and swim. (I didn't know how to swim, so I stayed in shallow water.) In high school, I played basketball and volleyball and was on the Pom-pom squad. So, I always kept busy. I remember growing up, we would go down south every summer. . . . I believe we would go to Mississippi, Louisiana, and Arkansas. And still, I never remember having talks about my mother. And I never asked questions about her.

There are questions I want to ask about my mother. I just don't know who to ask and when to ask. I want to know:

- How was she as a mother?
- Was she tidy or junky?
- What was her demeanor?
- How did she handle stress?
- Did she smoke or drink?
- What was her occupation?
- Did she graduate from high school?
- What did she do for fun?
- Did she ever express what she wanted me to do?

- Which sibling was closest to her?
- What were her last wishes?
- What were her flaws?
- Was she a believer?

Growing up, I never lacked love. While I have never—or let's say, I don't remember—anyone showing affection toward me by hugging me or telling me "I love you," the love I received was shown through how my family cared for me. I never lacked any material thing or food. Both sets of grandparents, aunts, uncles, and cousins all cared for me, so to me, that was love. So, of course, that shaped my beliefs about loving someone, caring for them, and treating them with respect. But there was still a void that no one could fill. And that was the void of a mother.

CHAPTER 2

A TWENTY-YEAR JOURNEY FOR A FOUR-YEAR DEGREE

Stop. Pause. Shift. Detour.
All things working together.
Delayed not denied.

"Yes, and from the ancient days, I am
he. No one can deliver out of my hand.
When I act, who can reverse it?"
Isaiah 43:13

Finish high school, go to college, earn a degree, and get a well-paying job. Oh, and by the way, if you didn't go to college, the military was your other option. Those were the instructions passed down from generation to generation. I'm sure you've heard this growing up. And great advice, might I add. The truth of the matter is that I wish I had experienced college life, especially the HBCU life. I missed out on the dorm life, and I always had a desire to be part of the D9 and go through that experience (I won't say which sorority). Yes, I know from others that college life has its ups and downs, but what part of life does not?

Not everyone chooses to go to college right after high school. Some choose to work, take up a trade, or enlist in the military. I had the opportunity to go to an HBCU, Mississippi Valley State University!! After touring MVSU, I just knew that's where I was headed. But later in my senior year of high school, I chose to enlist in the Army. I had sworn in and had my marching orders with a set date to leave for basic training. After a short few months of being sworn in, I had to make that difficult call to my recruiter to say, "Sir, I am pregnant." I was eighteen years old, and in my mind, the chances of the military or even going to college were slim to none. In hindsight, I could have gone to college with a baby, perhaps not Mississippi, but there are plenty of colleges in Milwaukee to choose from. But I made other choices.

The choices I made didn't include college until I was twenty years old. Yes, I know there are plenty of twenty-year-olds that have gone to HBCUs or other universities and experienced the "college life". However, my life was not set up like that. You see, I was not just a twenty-year-old. I was twenty years old, married, and had two toddlers. There was no way I could pull off any type of "college life". My first priority was making sure I could take care of my family. I knew that to get that well-paying job, I needed some sort of college education. So, I did what I felt was best for me at that moment and enrolled at a business college. I earned an Associate of Science degree from Bryant and Stratton College. Six months before graduating, I landed a part-time job in the corporate space as a secretary. After graduating, I stayed with the company and began working full-time. So, I checked all the boxes, right?

- ❑ Finish high school.
- ❑ Go to college.
- ❑ Earn a degree.
- ❑ Get a well-paying job.

Things were great!! At age twenty-two, I had an Associate of Science degree in information systems, and I had a great job with great benefits. With my associate's degree, I started my corporate career as a department secretary, then moved into a customer service rep role. From there I moved into information technology as a help desk analyst, which is how my career in technology started. I will talk more about my career in another chapter. All of this sounds great, right!? I was really off to a good start with my associate's degree, but that didn't seem to be enough for me.

Thinking back on my high school days, I remembered what a counselor told me at Milwaukee Tech High School. At Tech, I excelled in math and the electrical engineering shop class. My counselor advised me to take up electrical engineering as a trade, but, of course, I didn't listen. After all, "That's a field for boys," was my thinking. So, there I was reminiscing on that experience. I thought that maybe I could take what I have learned so far in the IT field and use it in engineering. I contacted an advisor at MSOE (Milwaukee School of Engineering), and I enrolled. What a joke!! I was so overwhelmed with intimidation that after one semester, I unenrolled at MSOE. At this point, I decided that college simply wasn't for me. For the next eleven or so years, I attended conferences, seminars, workshops, and corporate trainings to enhance my current role and keep myself marketable for the next advancement. By the grace of God, there was always advancement, yet I was not satisfied with my associate's degree and always yearned for more college education. I wanted that bachelor's degree, partly because others had one, and partly because I knew I would eventually need it for further career advancement.

After I dropped out of MSOE, I continued in my corporate career and went to every class I could to learn more about information technology. Then, I found my niche in the area of supporting technology. I continued to excel in my career and even moved up the ranks into leadership. As successful as I was in my career, that desire to go back to school would not leave my heart. I didn't know what I wanted out of a college degree; I just knew I wanted one. And finally, in 2002, I decided to go back to school.

During this time, I was living in Decatur, GA. I was working full-time, so I knew that whatever school I selected had to offer night school. In August 2002, I enrolled at DeVry University where I studied part-time for three years. Originally, I chose computer science as my major. After about a year, I switched my major to business administration with a focus on entrepreneurship. Now, I'm living the dream!! I have a good job, and I'm back in college. It's not an HBCU and I'm not living in a dorm, but I'm in college earning a bachelor's degree. I was actually living out my desire!!! And just like that, life happened, and it happened fast, and in 2005 I had to withdraw from school. Talk about a letdown!! For the next twelve years, I continued in my career. I took advantage of every training dollar available in my employer's budget. The goal was to remain marketable even without a bachelor's degree. And so, the journey continued without a bachelor's degree, but the desire to earn one never faded away.

So much life that happened in twelve years. The journey propelled me in a different direction in terms of higher education. I found myself at a crossroads and asked myself, "Do I go back to school and finish my business administration degree, or do I answer the pull to ministry?" In 2016, I journaled the following:

> ### October 14, 2016
> Ministry—I have a desire to go back to school for biblical counseling. I would love to be in a congregational care or life coaching position. Luther Rice is still burning in my spirit. I also want to teach more . . . teaching God's word. This helps me stay grounded and focused, and at the same time, it helps me to encourage and support others.

As one could imagine, I was stuck. I had no idea what to do. So, I decided to go back to college to finish my business administration degree. I hit a major roadblock: FINANCES!! How was I going to pay for school? On top of this, I owed a former school money so I couldn't even get my transcript from that school. Desire seemed to be shattered once again. Oh, but by the grace of God. . . .

"Life will bring your witness and faith into question." This was a quote from Pastor Cummings in a sermon that he preached on February 12, 2017. That quote described my very being at that exact moment. Everything about my life and what I believed God was telling me was in question. I chose my faith and put myself in position to allow the anointing of God to reconnect me, restore me, and revive me. The finances aligned, my transcript was released, and in August 2017, I began classes at Beulah Heights University (BHU).

For the next three years, I studied leadership and biblical studies at BHU. The leadership classes were useful for the marketplace and the church. Although I was thriving at BHU, something was unsettling. I was learning so much that helped me in the marketplace; however, I was thirsty to learn more of God's word, and I felt that was missing at BHU. After much fasting and praying, I withdrew and began taking classes at Point University in 2020. While studying Christian ministries at Point, I finally felt at peace about my degree program and about the path I was on. In June of 2022, I completed and earned a Bachelor of Science in Christian Ministries at Point University. This was all God's doing, and I'm so glad I followed the unction of the Holy Spirit to shift because Point has prepared me for the next phase of my education.

> # WHEN GOD PUTS DESIRES AND PURPOSE IN YOUR HEART, NO DELAY CAN THWART GOD'S PLAN UNLESS YOU ALLOW IT.

God will give you the desires of your heart even if it takes twenty years. It took me twenty years to complete a traditional four-year degree. Delay after delay, I finally earned a bachelor's degree at the magical age of fifty-two (five + two = seven . . . seven being the number of years for completion). Timing is everything, but in whose timing? Ecclesiastes tells us that there's a time for everything, including life's joys and life's sorrows. The delays we experience in life are either self-induced by our decisions or by things we have no control over. Delays teach us to be patient and to endure. Delays can be character builders and testers of our faith. When God puts desires and purpose in your heart, no delay can thwart God's plan unless you allow it. I don't care how long it takes, KEEP GOING!!! Philippians 2:13 (MSG) reminds us, "For it is [not your strength, but it is] God who is effectively at work in you, both to will and to work [that is, strengthening, energizing, and creating in you the longing and the ability to fulfill your purpose] for His good pleasure." And you know what? The desire for higher education continues. Remember that journal entry from October 14, 2016? Well, I thought I was in pursuit of that biblical counseling degree. After all, that is what I wrote, right?

In May 2022, I contacted Luther Rice and told the registrar that I was interested in registering for the MABC program (master of arts biblical counseling). I received all the paperwork, took the online orientation, and was ready to complete my application. I was eager and excited to enter this next phase.

"In their hearts humans plan their course, but the LORD establishes their steps" Proverbs 16:9 (NIV).

I was in the middle of reading the Bible, and it was as if He came and sat down next to me, and we began to have a conversation that went something like this:

God: What are you reading?

Me: I'm in Mark right now.

God: I know you've been wrestling with what master's program you should start.

Me: Yeah, I have been going back and forth between programs and schools.

God: What did you decide?

Me: Well, I decided on an MBA. I figured that I might as well pursue that to help me with my career.

God: You'll never be satisfied until you do what I called you to do.

Me: Yeah, but God, I thought I should pursue biblical counseling because that's what I wrote in my journal. But then I thought about it more. It doesn't make sense to pursue that since I have not done anything in that area, and I don't want a degree for the sake of just having a degree.

God: Well, I didn't tell you to pursue biblical counseling in the first place.

Me: God, in 2016, I wrote in my journal: "I have the desire to go back to school for biblical counseling." So now what?!!

God: So, fast forward and tell me what you wrote three years later. You remember that, right? Because THAT is what you actually pursued.

Me: Ughhh . . . I am so confused.

God: Listen, you wrote about biblical counseling, but I didn't tell you that. That was your desire. I told you about my desire for you, and you actually started it already. Until you do THAT, you'll never be satisfied.

After that conversation with God, I sat still and in deep thought. Over the next several weeks, I vacillated between a masters in biblical counseling, a master's of divinity, and masters of arts in leadership. The more I thought about biblical counseling the more unsettled I became, so I ruled that out. Remembering that conversation with God, I began to have peace about a Masters in Divinity (MDiv). I once again contacted the admissions office to inquire about the MDiv program. Just when I thought I had figured things out, I became unsettled again. And because I know that God is not a God of confusion, I went back to Him for answers. The MDiv is what I needed to continue the call to be a chaplain, which is what God told me in 2019. Hence my confusion. Then, the Holy Spirit directed me to look within my heart to reveal the one thing I am most passionate about: Leadership.

Ding, ding, ding, ding!!! I caught the revelation and went full steam ahead. Everything began to make sense. In this season, I am to be about my Father's business, which is leadership. When His business is about chaplaincy, I will shift. Once I got that aha moment and obediently changed my major, the rest of the process in enrolling into Luther Rice College and Seminary was seamless. Next up: Masters of Art in Leadership!!!

PRAYER:

Father God, I come against procrastination and stagnation. I come against the limited belief that is telling someone she is too old or it's too late for him to go back to school. Your time, Father God, is always the best time. You will get out of us what you destined for us even if we have to take a twenty-year journey. I release from the heavenly realm the finances needed for school. I pray for scholarships and grants to come forth in the name of Jesus. It could be a trade school, a business college, or a university. Whatever the certificate or degree may be, free that man or woman to yield and take that next first step. With you, God, it's never too late and we are never too old. In Jesus' name, I pray. Amen.

CHAPTER 3

PAYCHECK OR PURPOSE

The core of the heart.
Chosen by the industry.
Created for the call.

All I knew was that I loved to help people.

A career? What is that? The only work experience I had was working at Burger King and housekeeping at a hotel. I had no idea what I wanted as a career, I just knew I didn't want to flip burgers and be on fries or make beds and clean toilets.

Although I was in school earning an associate's degree, I didn't know what I was going to do with it. The degree was in information processing. It was a combination of administration, technology, and accounting. At twenty-one years old, I landed a part-time job in a major corporation. I was a department secretary in a training department, and I worked this job for six months until I graduated with my associate's degree.

The part-time job was the beginning of an amazing corporate career; however, during that time I didn't have a clue what I was doing or where I was headed in terms of a career. So, after I graduated, the company offered me a full-time job as a department secretary. The paycheck got bigger, and I was offered great benefits. There I was at twenty-two years old and working for one of the top corporations in Milwaukee. That was a big deal.

I worked as a department secretary for three years. Within those three years, I moved from the training department to human resources. It was in human resources that I began to understand my yearning to help people. My responsibilities called for people to reach out to me, and I had to research their questions to find the answers. I thoroughly enjoyed that aspect of my job, so when the opportunity was presented to work in our company's customer service department, I jumped at the chance. As a customer service rep, the need to help others was satisfied, and the paycheck got even bigger.

Although the job was feeding my satisfaction, customer service is not for the weak. You gotta have tough skin because people can be cruel. And you must be a bit touched to want to do this job day in and day out. Consider me touched because I loved it, and I was finding my place in the corporate world. Helping people solve their problems was my niche, and I enjoyed every bit of it. After working in this role for a year, I knew it was time for me to move on to something greater. The problem was that I didn't know what greater looked like. I just knew I felt a shift.

At this time, I was twenty-five years old. Although I believed in God and had accepted Jesus as my Lord and Savior, I didn't really have a relationship with Him. I mean, I prayed and went to church occasionally, but I didn't know how God's hand was really on me. I didn't know how he was working on my behalf and setting things in motion for me. I had boldness and courage, but I didn't know how that developed in me or where it came from, nor did I know that I was operating in crazy faith.

So, after a year of working in the customer service department, the crazy faith kicked into motion. I began to search for other opportunities within the company. Again, I didn't know where I was headed, I just knew it was time to do something different. A job opportunity titled "help desk analyst" was posted. I remember reading the job description and thinking, "I have no idea about working on computers, but I can learn if they give me a chance." Helping people solve problems appealed to me, so I applied for the position.

Remember, I had been a department secretary and a customer service rep. I had no business applying for a help desk analyst position where I would be troubleshooting and answering hardware and software questions . . . helping people with their computer problems. I was determined, and I waited and waited for a response. Finally, I got the call from human resources. The hiring manager wanted to talk to me.

The only thing I remember is telling the hiring manager that I believed I would be good for the job because I liked to help people. I didn't know anything about hardware or software. I didn't know anything about troubleshooting server or network problems. All I knew was that I was good at talking to people and I wanted to be in a position where I could help. I even remember saying how I was nice and always stayed calm even when customers yelled at me. LOL! "Ask and it will be given to you; seek and you will find; knock and the door will be opened to you" (Matthew 7:7, NIV). Well, the door opened, and I walked into the technology world carrying only the enjoyment of helping people. And guess what! The paycheck got even bigger. But something else was stirring up in me at the same time, and I could not put my finger on it.

I did not choose the technology field. The technology field chose me. I didn't go to school for computer science because I simply didn't know my career path. I didn't have a mentor to help me figure that out. I just knew I wanted greater. And in that wanting greater, unbeknownst to me, my purpose began to take shape. I had to go through years of wandering before it all made sense. In those wandering years, my paychecks got bigger, and the revelation of purpose became more evident.

All I knew was that I loved to help people. But in what capacity?

I cannot explain how the door opened in my career other than it was all God's doing. After working as a help desk analyst for five years, my career in the computer support environment took off. In 1999, I moved to Atlanta, GA on a job transfer to help start up the help desk, and I found myself in a leadership role. Why? All because I love to help people, and for the next twenty-four years, I functioned as a technical support leader. The paychecks kept getting bigger and my purpose continued to elevate.

> I'M ALMOST POSITIVE HAD I DEVELOPED A RELATIONSHIP WITH GOD YEARS AGO, MY EYES WOULD HAVE BEEN OPENED TO MY PURPOSE.

As a technical support leader, I have worked in the HVAC space, local government space, healthcare technology space, and cyber security space. I have a vast skillset that I am grateful for; however, you don't hear me talking about my career or skillsets because my fulfillment rests in the people I have served . . . the people I have led and the customers I have helped. I thoroughly enjoy the increase of coins in my bank account. But what has given me the most satisfaction are the seeds I have planted along the way.

Jeremiah 29:11 (NIV) says, "For I know the plans I have for you," declares the Lord, "plans to prosper you and not to harm you, plans to give you hope and a future." If you keep reading, you'll see in verse 13 where the Lord says through the prophet Jeremiah, "You will seek me and find me when you seek me with all your heart." Although this was all in a letter written by Jeremiah to the exiles in Babylon, we can take this same letter and apply it to our lives. I'm almost positive had I developed a relationship with God years ago, my eyes would have been opened to my purpose. But God is so gracious and patient. And He gave me yet another chance. . . .

PRAYER:

Thanks be to the God of a second chance. Almighty God, we often mistreat your word that tells us that you have a plan and purpose for our lives. While your word is true, we often allow our circumstances to distract us from hearing you; and therefore, we miss the call. I come to you with a humble spirit on behalf of those seeking clarity and understanding of the purpose of their existence. Grant him or her the wisdom to discern the path you have laid out for their life, the strength to overcome challenges, and the courage to embrace the lessons that come their way. Illuminate their mind with the light of knowledge and purpose, so that they may see beyond the mundane and grasp the deeper meaning of their journey. Guide each person in using their unique gifts and talents to contribute positively to the world and fulfill the purpose you have envisioned for them. Grant each of us patience in times of uncertainty, and may our actions be guided by love, compassion, and a genuine desire to make a meaningful impact.

GOD IS PRETTY GOOD AT SECOND CHANCES

In moments of doubt, remind us that we are a part of a greater plan, intricately woven into the tapestry of existence. Father God, may our lives be a reflection of your divine purpose and may each of us find fulfillment in aligning our will with yours. In the name of Jesus I pray, Amen.

CHAPTER 4

THE CALL AND THE RESPONSE

Ringing in the ear.
A blank stare. Ignored. Running.
It's in the answer.

JOURNAL ENTRY

November 15, 2011

I woke up this morning with my mind stayed on Jesus. I called a dear friend and his mother this morning. It was good to speak to them. It was good to hear his voice and to know that he is still working and trying to resist the temptations of using drugs. The devotion: I Thessalonians 5:18 and Psalm 107:1 (NKJV): "Oh, give thanks unto the Lord for He is good, For His mercy endures forever." Today was another filled day. Filled with God's presence, God's word, and God's people. Today I celebrate life. I saw someone give herself to Christ . . . born again . . . a new life. Today we built our fifth house for a young lady with four kids. As we prayed over her and her new home, the presence of God filled the atmosphere, and a life was saved. Hallelujah!! This lady was HIV positive, so we prayed for her HIV to be healed. Lord, I ask that you show me/ tell me my true purpose. What is it that you want me to do? Counseling and foster care

are heavily on my heart. What is it, Lord, that you have called me to do? I want to do your will. I want to be lined up with you. Sociology is the degree I want to pursue. And then go into counseling. Help me, Father God!!"

The above was a journal entry from my first mission trip to Nairobi, Kenya in 2011. This was an experience of a lifetime that helped to catapult my call into ministry. It was on this mission trip that I felt God pulling me more and more toward ministry work. No blinking neon lights were saying, "*THIS WAY!*", so of course I didn't have a clue what I was supposed to be doing in ministry. It took many years, a lot of tears, and a lot of peeling back layers before awareness began to take shape. Even in the unknowing, I continued to serve in the church, and it was serving in the church that offered self-discovery.

In 2012, I went on the Walk to Emmaus (a spiritual retreat). Here is where I began to learn how to receive Jesus' love through other people. It was during this retreat that I began to understand that I am the hands and feet of Jesus, and Jesus is counting on me to work God's mission. One of the best pieces of advice came while on this retreat. One of the spiritual leaders said to me, "Raquel, you know what you know, now allow your heart to receive it." This was heavy!! It was time that my heart and mind lined up with each other. It was time to operate in faith.

One thing God revealed to me on this retreat was that I was not to take an assignment in a certain ministry. I went back and told my pastor that I couldn't serve in the capacity asked of me. And I remember him saying something like, "But Emmaus is to help you understand serving." I told him that Emmaus did help me understand serving but not in that capacity. Soon after the Emmaus journey, I became a Stephen Minister where I was providing Christian/spiritual care for women in the congregation. The journey in ministry was beginning to take shape on the trajectory toward Christian counseling.

JOURNAL ENTRY

November 15, 2011

Perseverance: "Stand Firm During the Bumpy Times"

Be self-controlled and alert. Your enemy the devil prowls around like a roaring lion looking for someone to devour. Resist him, standing firm in the faith, because you know that your brothers throughout the world are undergoing the same kind of sufferings (I Peter 5:8-9, author paraphrase). While on the mission trip in Kenya, I had a lot of up and down emotional moments. I saw more poverty than I had ever witnessed in my life. What frustrated me the most were the bumps and potholes in the roads. I was tired of being "shaken up". I kept thinking, "Lord, why?" and "I cannot deal with the roads." And once I even thought, "I can't do this at all." Today the Holy Spirit arrested me and reminded me that the people here have to deal with these roads every single day, and all God is asking me to give is three to four days. Then I can go back home to my "smooth streets". Yesterday, we got stuck in the mud for the second time this week, and I admit that I was so frustrated. Even today, the roads are bumpy, but the frustration level did not rise. When we got to the muddy spots, I simply went into prayer. When the Holy Spirit arrested me, He told me that the bumps and potholes in the road represent life. I will continue to have bumps and potholes in the road for as long as I am living, and I possibly may even get stuck. I may be able to dodge some, but others I will have to cross and go through. He said the blessing in them is that I have Christ Jesus to lean on. The Holy Spirit also said that when I get stuck in muddy situations, Jesus will surround me with the right circle of influence to encourage me, guide me, and push me out. Praise be to God! Galatians 6:9 (NIV) says, "Let us not become weary in doing good, for at the proper time we will reap a harvest if we do not give up." What if I had told Fred that I was giving up and could do no more? What if any of us gave up in a tough situation? We would have missed our blessing, and we would miss blessing someone else through our witness and testimony.

"Perseverance" was the second journal entry written on the same day while in Kenya in 2011. Why is it significant now? As I look back over the years, I had to persevere during all my internal and external struggles, while at the same time understand my call to ministry. I had to fight through self-sabotage as liquor was becoming my way to cope. I also had to deal with the false beliefs that were planted: rejection, abandonment, and not being good enough.

The journey of discovering my spiritual gifts and understanding my call continued, and so did the personal transformation. I continued to serve, and I found myself yearning for God more and more. I wanted to read more, study more, and just be in God's presence. I began taking different Bible study classes at church and studying on my own.

In 2016, I found myself back in Kenya on another mission assignment. The assignment was similar to the first mission: build homes, feed and minister to the street boys, and fellowship with the elders. This go around, something was stirring up in me that hadn't the first time. I was bolder and more courageous as I talked about Jesus to people, and the compassion I already had for people was strengthened. I remember filling bags with corn for the elders. As we were filling the bags, one of the pastors asked me to pray over each bag as we placed them in the pickup area. I remember thinking, "I don't know what I'll be doing, but I know I'll be serving people by being with them and talking to them and listening to them." The more I prayed, the more I felt strongly connected to God. In this same year, I wrote my personal vision statement and my personal motto.

Vision Statement: To comfort those who are suffering and to support others in their joys and victories.

Personal Motto: Life isn't meant to be traveled alone.

For the next three years, I went on a personal mission to study and pray as much as I could because I knew God had something for me, and I had to find out what it was.

JOURNAL ENTRY
February 19, 2018
There is so much on my mind. So many things I want to do, go, get done. Two promises I'm standing on are:

Delighting myself in the Lord, and He'll give me the desires of my heart (Psalm 37:4).

> Seeking first the kingdom of God and His righteousness and all these things will be added to me (Matthew 6:33).
>
> Lord, I want <u>your</u> will for me. Are these desires from you or are they fleshly?
>
> I want to start my CPE classes.
>
> I want to go to school full-time.

Did I start those CPE classes? And did I go to school full-time? I sure did. . . . I did both. On June 17, 2019, I wrote a one-sentence journal entry: "Hospital chaplaincy is in my future because I have been called to this ministry." I remember this time so vividly. It was a month after I had broken my ankle, and I was ready and eager to journal all that was on my mind, and so I wrote that one-liner, and froze. Nothing else flowed. There were no more words. The only thing I could do was stare at that one sentence and read it over and over again. And then I did all I knew to do at the moment . . . pray. Nine days later, I received an email offering me the intern training position for hospital chaplaincy. Fast forward, I started my chaplain residency in 2020 and completed it in 2021. (Delight yourself in the Lord and he will give you the desires of your heart. . . . Seek first the kingdom of God and his righteousness and all these things will be added to you.) And oh, by the way, I went to school full-time from 2020-2022.

MANY RECEIVE THEIR CALL TO MINISTRY BUT ONLY A FEW ANSWER THE CALL.

Matthew 22:14 (NKJV) says, "For many are called, but few are chosen." "The many called" embrace all who hear the gospel—the whole Jewish nation, and the Gentiles of every land where the gospel is preached. The chosen are those who choose to accept. Tony Evans says it this way,

> *Those who don't utilize what God has pro-*
> *vided and fail to be faithful servants will*
> *lose out on full participation in the millen-*
> *nial kingdom. As a result, they will expe-*
> *rience profound regret. Many are called*
> *to receive salvation because of their faith*

*in Christ Jesus, but only a few are chosen
because of their unfaithfulness.*[2]

Many receive their call to ministry but only a few
answer the call. Even when you don't understand the
assignment . . . even when you don't see the "how"
. . . even when you are afraid . . . even when you don't
understand the "why"—answer the call and allow
God to orchestrate His plan for you.

After that year as a resident chaplain, I returned
to a corporate leadership role. God has rewarded me
with a role exceedingly abundantly more than I could
have asked for or imagined. This was just another
pit stop that will continue to shape me for the next
assignment. God gave me a chance to taste my call.

Answering God's call to ministry doesn't always
mean that you'll walk into its manifestation over-
night. I fully accepted my call into ministry in February 2017. On May 21, 2023, I became ordained
and licensed as a minister at the church that I attend
and serve: Stronghold Christian Church. I am in a
preparation season and getting fully equipped for the
call of a chaplain.

---

2 Tony Evans, *CSV Tony Evans Study Bible* (Nashville, TN: Holman Bible Publishers,
2019), commentary section.

I am learning to exercise more patience on this journey, and I'm learning how to endure and perservere better. I encourage you to do the same. There are some things you may have to do, and those things could take five, ten, or even twenty years to complete. Are you willing to take the journey? How committed will you be to fulfilling your call? You'll only see the second chance if you're willing to do the work.

CHAPTER 5

DIVORCED BUT NOT DENIED LOVE

Patience. Faith. Hope. Kindness.
March twenty-third. Two thousand nineteen.
Love wins again.

Forget the former things; do not dwell on
the past. See I am doing a new thing! Now
it springs up; do you not perceive it?
Isaiah 43:18-19 (NIV)

On December 31, 1987, I took on a new identity. I was eighteen years old and pregnant with my first child. For the next twenty-one years, eleven months, and twenty-nine days, I was married and known as Raquel Watts. Not all of these years were bad; in fact, there were many, many great years. However, the trials outweighed the good, and my first marriage ended on December 30, 2009.

During my first marriage, I lived life like I saw it. I made sure I took care of my husband and my children. I cared for others when they were in need, but I never stopped to know me. Externally, life was really good at times. Internally, I was a mess. I lived loveless with undisclosed anger, resentment, and envy. I looked for love and attention in the wrong places and with the wrong people. Over the years, anger became my defense mechanism. I slowly drifted away and became emotionally unattached. At that time, I had no idea why I felt detached. That discovery came later. (Refer to chapter 1.) In April

2009, I knew the marriage was finally over, and so I began my exit strategy. Little did I know what was waiting for me. . . .

I had gotten married at eighteen years of age, and now at forty years of age, I found myself alone and in a very dark place. I wanted out of the marriage, but I wasn't prepared for the road ahead. So, there I was divorced and living alone, and the first one and a half years were pure torture. The torture was from within as I battled depression and wondered if life was even worth living.

During this time, I joined a church that saved my life holistically. I was spiritually dead, mentally exhausted, and on the path of physical destruction. St. James United Methodist Church in Alpharetta, GA became my spiritual hospital. It was here that I re-dedicated my life to Christ and our relationship took off. It was just me and Jesus. It was here that I took my first Bible study class, "Shattering Strong-holds". The process of peeling back layers to uncover the root of anger, envy, and detachment had begun, and this was just the beginning.

It was also at St. James where I became naked and unashamed. And it was at that moment of being stripped down that God was able to do a new work in me. A year after the divorce, I went to Kenya on a mission assignment, and that assignment turned my perspective on life "upside right". Everything I was going through became minuscule. I still battled, but I stayed in the fight. In the years to follow, I began to seek God's face instead of His hand, I began to see people differently, and I began to know and love myself in a way that I have never experienced. It was in this journey that I discovered self-love.

In the midst of this transformation, I met my now husband, Tim, in 2014. We met on a dating website. We sure did!!! And we talked for two weeks before we met face-to-face. Now, two years prior to meeting Tim, I had written, "God, this is what I want in my mate" letter. That letter was short-lived because while I was on a spiritual retreat, the Holy Spirit instructed me to throw the letter out. He asked me, "Do you actually think your creation is better than my creation?" Wowsers!! When I got home from that retreat, I balled up the letter and threw it in the trash.

Now when I first saw Tim, my mind went to that letter I had written. I thought, "he's dark and handsome, but he's not tall. . . . two out of three ain't bad." LOL!! The next two years involved a lot of discovery about each other while we continued to heal from our first marriages. I had been divorced for five years, and Tim had been divorced for four years. We were both still healing while at the same time open to a new relationship.

True story. There was a time in our courtship when we split up for about six months. Neither of us was ready to take the relationship further, so we called it quits . . . or so we thought. I had really grown fond of Tim, and I missed his friendship. I found out that one of his pastors was coming to my church to preach. So, I went fishing. I texted Tim and told him that his pastor was scheduled to preach at my church at the upcoming Wednesday night service. He took the bait, and I reeled him in. We continued dating, and our relationship grew stronger. On May 12, 2018, we got engaged and on March 23, 2019, we were introduced as Mr. and Mrs. Timothy Copeland.

IF YOU ARE CONSIDERING REMARRIAGE, BE AWARE OF THE STUMBLING BLOCKS IN YOUR PAST AND YOUR PRESENT.

In spite of my many mess-ups in my first marriage, God granted me the desires of my heart, and that was to marry a godly man. Not a perfect man, but a man who loved God. A man with a servant's heart. But you need to know this came at a cost. I had to die to my internal barriers. I had to reconcile with God, forgive my first husband, and forgive myself. None of which was easy to do. I had to let go of the past and open my hand to the future. I had to face all my ugliness and work on myself before I could offer my authentic self to anyone. I had to grow in patience, kindness, and love.

If you are considering remarriage, be aware of the stumbling blocks in your past and your present. Be aware of external barriers, and most importantly, your internal barriers. Deal with your baggage!! Allow God to transform your good, your bad, and your ugly because in all things He works for the good of those who love him, who have been called according to his purpose (see Romans 8:28). When you find yourself contemplating a second marriage, (or even your first marriage), know that with patience, understanding, communication, hard work, and love, you can walk into your new beginning!

*Love is patient and kind; love does not envy or
boast; it is not arrogant or rude. It does not insist
on its own way; it is not irritable or resentful;
it does not rejoice at wrongdoing but rejoices
with the truth. Love bears all things, believes
all things, hopes all things, endures all things.*
1 Corinthians 13:4-7 (ESV)

PRAYER:

*Loving and gracious God, many are grappling
with the pain and confusion that accompanies
the journey of divorce. Grant them the strength
to navigate these tumultuous waters with grace
and resilience. Help them find peace in the midst
of chaos and clarity in the midst of uncertainty.
As they face the challenges of letting go, guide
them towards forgiveness—both for others and
for themselves. Let your love be a balm for their
wounds, soothing the ache that resides deep
within. Lord God may understanding replace
bitterness and may compassion be the driving
force in every interaction. During moments of*

loneliness and despair, remind someone that your love is unwavering and ever-present. Help them to discover their own strength and resilience, knowing that they are not defined by divorce. Grant healing to the broken places and renewal to their wounded spirit. Father God, for the person contemplating the possibility of entering into a new chapter of marriage, grant them wisdom to discern the path that aligns with your divine plan for their life. Help them to see beyond their own desires or fears, seeking a union that is built on love, understanding, and shared purpose. If there are lessons from the past that they need to carry, grant them the strength to learn and grow from them. Let the scars of previous experiences be reminders of resilience, not barriers to future happiness. Above all, Lord God, give them peace and assurance knowing they are walking in alignment with your will. In Jesus' name I pray, Amen.

BLOOMING: GOD MADE DIRT AND DIRT DON'T HURT

They say. You say. Who?
Identity. Core. Within.
I am. Her. She. Me.

Let me introduce myself. I am a wife, a mother, and a grandmother. I am a daughter, a granddaughter, a sister, and an aunt. I am a niece and a cousin to many. I am a friend to some and an acquaintance to others. I am a volleyball player, a basketball player, and a cheerleader. I am a cheerleading coach and a team mom. I am an administrator, a life coach, a chaplain, and a corporate leader. I am this. . . . and I am that.

Truth is, I have allowed some of these roles and titles to define me . . . to give me my identity. Throughout my life, I got so wrapped up in the performance of the roles that I only knew myself on a surface level. The true essence of my being was unknown. In Matthew 16:13, 15 (author paraphrase), Jesus asked his disciples, "Who do they say I am?" He then asked, "Who do YOU say I am?" For years—many, many years—I lived a life of being God's acquaintance. I never knew Him for myself. My knowledge of Him was second-handed and so was my faith. Once I began to have a relationship with God, I began to know him as Mother, Father, Provider, Healer, and Comforter.

Little did I know, I was only an acquaintance of myself. It took a divorce at the age of forty to begin the self-discovery. There were a lot of dark times, and I hated being alone. Why? Because God was showing me her, and I didn't like her at all. I didn't like who she was and what she was becoming. Was this really me? Was I really the person whom God created? Or was I a product of circumstances and self-destruction? So, I spent many nights alone dealing with me.

After about the fifteenth "God if you get me out of this, I promise to never . . .", life began to shift. I truly surrendered, and God was then able to do a new work in me. I started to fall in love with me. But there was still a small problem. Loving me was one thing but knowing me was a whole other something else. I had to ask myself, "Raquel, who do they say you are?" And after I made the list of all the things people would say about me, I then asked, "Raquel, who do YOU say you are?"'

I WOULD ARGUE THAT WHEN YOU KNOW WHO YOU ARE AND WHOSE YOU ARE, TRANSITIONS MAY BE A BIT EASIER TO NAVIGATE.

I was well into my forties before I could answer the latter. You see, when you don't take the time to know yourself, you live a life for others. This is one reason why many parents have a hard time moving on in life when they become empty nesters. This is why divorcees move on to the next marriage so quickly. This is why many retirees return to work. Their life was defined by their roles as mother, father, wife, husband, or laborer. And when seasons end or shift, they lose themselves and often ask, "Now what do I do?" I would argue that when you know who you are and whose you are, transitions may be a bit easier to navigate.

Who are you? What are your core values? What is your belief system? What do you enjoy doing? What are your dislikes? What are your bad habits? What are your good habits? What stresses you out? How do you cope with stress? What comes easy to you? What are your challenges? What gives you satisfaction? What makes your heart smile? What makes you sad? When you don't know yourself, you make allowances for anything to happen. So yeah, I had to sit with myself. And in all that ugliness, pain, and discomfort, things got real.

GOD IS PRETTY GOOD AT SECOND CHANCES

The best way to know someone is to spend time with them, right? So that's what I did. I spent time with myself, and I discovered that I really like me. I began going to the movies alone, going to dinner alone, and I even started going to the park alone. At the park, I would walk and pray, or I would simply sit on the bench and journal. My favorite spot at that time was Morgan Falls in Roswell, GA. I sat on the swing bench and stared out into the Chattahoochee River. That's the place where I did a lot of writing and wondering. The more I dated myself, the more I fell in love with me, and the more I got to know myself. The more I got to know myself, I was able to give myself an identity.

I don't want it to seem as though this journey of self-discovery was easy because it definitely was not. It took a lot of time, tears, and intentionality to take off the false persona and replace it with authenticity. And once the self-discovery took place, I then had to own who I really was. I had to own my values and belief systems. I had to be comfortable in my own skin and in vocalizing who I was. I had to stop dumbing down my accomplishments and victories. After all, every hurdle I got over, every fear I faced, every mountain I climbed, and every second chance was all done by the grace of God. To talk about it is to glorify God as a testament to just how good He is at second chances. And today, you cannot explain me, and I cannot explain myself if the supernatural is left out. I am but a tool of God. So . . .

Allow me to re-introduce myself.

My name is Roc, oh, R-to-the-O-C

No, no . . . I'm kidding, but seriously. I am Minister Raquel Copeland. Before anything, I am a child of God the Father and a disciple of Jesus Christ. I am holy because God is holy, and I am set apart for God's purpose. I hold firm the virtues of love, compassion, encouragement, and authenticity. I am an introvert, refueled and rejuvenated when I sit alone. At my core, I am a server. I love to help others and watch them transform. I love to help others make the best out of their circumstances. It is through self-awareness that I discovered my personal vision statement: To Comfort Those Who Are Suffering and To Support Others In Their Joys and Victories.

I am the Founder and CEO of SoJourn Coaching, LLC. I have over twenty years of experience in non-profit, for-profit, and government organizations in the areas of technology, leadership, mentoring, strategic planning, coaching, and training. I bring many years of church leadership, facilitation, and local and international missionary experience. I have earned an Associate of Science degree in information processing from Bryant and Stratton College and a Bachelor of Science degree in Christian Ministries from Point University. At the time of this writing, I am working toward a Master of Arts in leadership from Luther Rice College and Seminary. I have earned leadership certificates in a variety of corporate trainings, including Six Sigma Greenbelt. I have earned five units of clinical pastoral education from The Institute for Spiritual Health and Wellness at Chris180. I am a published author, an ordained and licensed minister to preach the gospel, an ICF-certified professional coach through Dream Releaser Coaching, and I am a certified pre-marital facilitator through SYMBIS.

I list these roles and accomplishments not to define who I am, but only to brag on God and to illustrate just how good He is at second chances.

HAIKUS— SEPTEMBER 2021

Remember the camping excursion in September 2021 that I spoke about? Here are several more Haikus I penned while seated at the campsite, appreciating the beauty of God's creation.

LET THERE BE
The good creation.
Humanity and nature.
Connecting as one.

THE ANSWER
Be calm. Nature calls.
Connect. Listen. Small whispers.
Be still. Hear God's voice.

WEBS OF LIFE
Beautifully crafted.
Spawned to trap and entangle.
Careful. Don't get caught.

DIRTY MATTERS
Deep. Dark. Messy. Heavy.
A little on never hurts.
Required for growth.

BRIGHT FUTURE
Count the promises.
Impossible. Too many.
Blessed beyond measure.

HYDRATE
Springs. Streams. Lakes. Rivers.
To live requires tasting.
Never thirst again.

KEEP GOING!!

Printed in the USA
CPSIA information can be obtained
at www.ICGtesting.com
LVHW010734220324
775204LV00015B/1140